In God's Time

*To Sora
Antionette

-T-T Bona

from Rebera E Foston-comor
7/96*

Rebera Elliott Foston, M.D., MPH

Forward

In this my fourth published work, I would again like to thank Almighty God for continuing to bless me with the gift of poetry, and for using me as a vessel to share the pain of the children.

I would like to thank my husband, Will, for continuing to support my dream at the cost of some of his own

My sons, Bryan and Amia, for continuing to understand my need to follow my dream, as they dream dreams of their own

My mother, the late Mrs. Erma Elliott, and my father, the late Mr. Frank Elliott for continuing to cheer for me from the front row, but just from higher seats

My sisters and brother, for continuing to be proud of me

My uncles, aunts, and cousins for enjoying my work

My Godmother, Mary Coplen, who has nurtured me for almost twenty-four years

My God sisters, Tanya, Lillian, Phyllis, my God brothers Tyrone, and the late Thomas Coplen for keeping me down to earth

My Godsons, Jimmy, Daud, and Raphael for continuing to inspire me with their courage

My Goddaughters, Lori, Elizabeth, Allyson, Michelle, and my sorors, Camille, Lawanda, and Shanice, for continuing to encourage me with their friendship

The Butler Family, especially Mary, Cleotis, and Regina for making me feel so special

But most of all I would like to thank the thousands of teenagers who continue to touch my life, even though their cries are still being lost to the night

Table of Contents

Introduction

Rebera Elliott Foston, M.D., MPH has always liked to write poetry. She managed to include some creative writing courses in her studies at Fisk University, but her passion for writing soon became overshadowed by her technical studies. She graduated Magna Cum Laude, Phi Beta Kappa, in Biology from Fisk. Then she received her medical degree from Meharry Medical College in Nashville, and her Masters Degree in Public Health from the University of North Carolina, in Chapel Hill. She became a Board Certified Family Practitioner, with an emphasis in Adolescent Health Care, and received her Post Doctoral training in Family Medicine, at Michigan State University, in East Lansing. She was the first female Health Commissioner for the City of Gary, Indiana, where she was born and reared.

Her passion for writing poetry, however, reemerged shortly after she dedicated her practice of medicine to "Adolescents Only" in 1985. In that same year she created the Foston Adolescent Workshop, Inc. where she has helped over 1800 teenagers feel good about themselves by giving them the time, space, and latitude to hone their musical, writing, acting, speaking, critical thinking, and caring skills. However, it was after she had heard and treated the real pain of over 15,000 teenage patients and their parents, that she decided to try to capture some of this pain on paper. Already thousands of teenagers have heard and been visibly touched by her poetry.

Dr. Foston's current goal is to create a home that can house hundreds of teenagers who find themselves not being parented. This home will be called "Somewhere" (There Is A Place For Us). A portion of the proceeds from this book as from all of the Foston Adolescent Workshop projects will be directed toward making this goal a reality.

Dr. Rebera Elliott Foston would like for you to read and hopefully enjoy this manuscript. She hopes that some poem or passage may touch you, help you, heal you, amuse you, strengthen you, or move you in some way.

Will Foston, M.D.

Chapter One

The Validation

In God's Time

I've been looking for you
for a while now
What I have to tell you
I will try to be kind

but you need to

>Stop your cravin'
>Stop your scathin'
>Stop your wavin'
>Stop your ravin'

'Cause everything happens
In God's time

It happens

>In God's space
>In God's hand
>In God's place
>In God's plan

Everything happens
In God's time...

Control

I greeted you
with warmth
You treated me
so cold
I cowered in fear
You acted
more bold

I shared with you
my dreams
and me, you would
then scold
I was honest
and true
while you played
a role

I offered you
my love
to have and
to hold
I gave you
my heart
but you wanted
my soul

I gave you part
of my life
but you wanted
the whole
All you
really wanted
was complete
CONTROL

Who's Who

Yes, you can be so sweet
and charming
it is true

But usually
I can't figure out
what is wrong with you

One day you'll buy me
something that is
all shiny and new

Then the next day,
you will beat me
until I'm black and blue

The next morning you'll
say you're sorry
and stick to me like glue

That night, you'll
beat me again,
knowing our baby is due

Good friends, you have
made quite sure
I have only a few

You try to keep me
so isolated that
I don't know what to do

When I look into your
face, I don't have
the slightest clue

People should have one
personality, but here
you are with two

The devil or the
man I married, Today,
which one are you?

I stay so upset
because I can't tell
anymore who's who!

Every Monday

For as long as I can remember
I have always wanted to teach
I thought with patience and love
some children I could reach

At first I had so much joy
teaching kids that were not that smart
knowing I was helping some child
get off to the right start

But, I can't do this much longer
No one warned me I could feel this way
but, you should hear what I have to hear
Lord, every Monday!

One child told me how he got a big bruise
another one hadn't slept
One hadn't eaten all weekend
while another just sat and wept

One child's hair hadn't been combed
another had really bad breath
One seemed wired on something
while another seemed bored to death

One child smelled of cheap alcohol
another one smelled of "weed"
One just wanted to talk about sex
while another on himself, he peed

One child came in very late
and to me, he looked the worst
but then I remembered, he's always like that
the Monday after the "first"

I don't know how much more of this
I can actually stand
When my own life is in shambles
Shoot, I don't even have me a man

But, if I give up people will talk
and I know exactly what they will say
"She called herself a teacher
She was just in it for the pay!"

But they don't see what I see
or know about the things I pray
and they don't walk into my "preschool" class
Lord, every Monday!

My Question

I've heard you tell your girlfriends
You don't need a man in your life
and how you don't even care
If you are never someone's wife

I have heard you say it so often
But, if what you say is true
then Mama, I think I have something
I really need to ask you

You taught me how to ride my bike
and showed me how to catch a ball
You paid for my music lessons
and made me stand straight and tall

You cut the grass, wash the car
and take out all the trash
You take me to all of my baseball games
If you have to make a mad dash

You tuck me into my bed at night
Stay with me until I fall asleep
and when you say, we'll do something
That's a promise, I know you will keep

When you buy me a present
I know it will be just the right size
I know I will see you every day
so with you there is no surprise

You take me to church every Sunday
and you taught me how to pray
You help me with my homework
'Til it's done, I can't go out to play

You yell at me when I've done wrong
and then you spank my butt
Each time you spank me, you also make sure
I know exactly for what

Whenever someone tries to hurt me
You are the first to step in
You taught me how to fight
and how to graciously win

But from what I've learned in school
and always see on TV
That in a "real family"
There're usually at least three

There's supposed to be a mother, a father
and then they have a child
So, there's something I've wanted to ask you
and I've wanted to know for quite a while

You say I ask too many questions
Please, let me ask just one more
Mama, if you do all those things for me
Then, tell me, What's a Daddy for?

Why Now?

You never came
to see him
or even called him
on the phone

When you would
see him in public
You never let on
that he was your own

You never wished him
Happy Birthday
or watched him play
one football game

So why are you
standing here now
calling out
his name?

You never even bought
him one present
or on a test
wished him good luck

Or helped him with
one homework problem
all those times when
he would get stuck

You never checked
on his work at school
or in the hospital
when he pulled up lame

So why are you
standing here just
now calling
out his name?

You never once
said you were sorry
when you stood him up
each and every time

Or even bailed him
out of jail
when he started
committing those crimes

I know that
after today
Nothing will ever
be the same

I'll remember the first
time you kissed him
After standing there
calling out his name

He was trying
to be like you
I mean like the man
you have never been

You say that
you are so sorry
Well, don't tell me
You better tell him

But you know that
he can't hear you
He's only fifteen and
you know who's to blame

That's why you are
hanging off his coffin
and just now
calling out his name

Daddy's Little Girl

When you are young
You should be happy
filled with excitement
and glee
like everyone having
a good time
while trimming the
Christmas tree

"You know how moody
that child can be,"
is all that I would
hear them say
But my daddy would tell them
"She's my little girl,
Ya'll shouldn't tease
her that way!"

For years I would be
so upset, the slightest
thing could
make me cry
It almost drove me
out of my mind
Just trying to
figure out why

I had to know why
I was so different
from the rest
of my family
I had to go
deep inside my
mind to solve
this mystery

At first the
pieces of my
memories seemed faint
and badly scattered
Like a lovely vase
that's mishandled and
ends up broken
and shattered

Slowly then painfully
images formed that
were blurred and
sometimes dim
A shadow kept coming
into my bedroom
One night I realized
it was him!

He must have thought
I was my Mama
the way he touched
and kissed my face
But I knew he was more
than drunk when
he forced himself
into my "special place"

No one will ever
know how badly
I wanted and
needed to scream
When I realized that
what had happened
was real and not just
a bad dream

All of my memories
are back together
now all of the
pieces fit
But, to this day
I'm not quite sure
which one of them
I want to hit

My Mama, for not caring
or believing and
for making me feel
all of the guilt
Or him for being
an alcoholic and
those nights climbing
under my quilt

Even though he
cursed her, messed
with me, and all of us
he battered
My Mama acted like
keeping a man
in her bed was all
that really mattered

Well, today I'm rocking
and nursing my child
and a thought keeps
shaking my world
Because my Daddy
wouldn't stay in my
Mama's bed, I'm holding
Daddy's little girl!

Christmas In July

Have we forgotten something?
I know, a Christmas card
I don't care what the neighbors say
I want Santa lit up in the yard

Let's hurry and put up more decorations
It will be hard but we have to try
I know it seems unusual
having Christmas in July

But please don't ask me why
I just have something in my eye

Help me wrap up all of her presents
in this shiny wrapping paper
Let's put up the artificial tree
and spray with that pine scented vapor

I've got a turkey in the oven
and her favorite sweet potato pie
See how much fun it will be
having Christmas in July

I said don't ask me why
Stand still while I straighten your tie

See, we can use white cotton
and pretend that it is snow
We will light up all the candles
and give the room a soft glow

Now for her special present
Let's see, what shall we buy
Oh yes, a beautiful dress
for her Christmas in July

You just can't ask me why
because I am trying not to cry

I've invited all of the family
No one can make it, it seems
The three of us will have extra helpings
is all it really means

You are so young , how did you guess it
I'm okay that was just a relief sigh
Yes, my child from this AIDS thing
your younger sister will surely die

That's why we are having Christmas in July
Please help me say Good-bye

Chapter Two

The Commisuration

In God's Time

...Who do I think I am?
My advice to you seems out of line

I just know you need to

> Stop your worryin'
> Stop your flurryin'
> Stop your scurryin'
> Stop your hurryin'

'Cause everything happens
In God's Time

It happens

> In God's base
> In God's way
> In God's face
> In God's day

Everything happens
In God's Time...

He Said , She Said

Boy, my friend Lisa told me that
around the corner you led
a little girl in high school
who wore her hair in "dreds"

She told me when she called
your name, the two of you then fled
What's that red stuff on your collar?
Don't tell me that you bled

Girl, to your accusations
Not guilty I have pled
Because you know for evidence
You do not have a shred

Now girl, you know that up
with you, I am getting fed
Because here you go with some old
He Said, She Said

Well, my friend Lisa told me
She saw you coming out of the shed
You said you were looking for oats
for your new thoroughbred

But you told me you were going
to the store to get some bread
Boy, if you are lying to me
May God strike you dead

Girl, how do you keep
all this stuff inside your head
Again the tiniest evidence
you do not have a shred

And up with you again
I am getting fed
You gonna step to me with
that old He Said, She Said

But my friend Lisa told me
that she caught you in bed
last night with some old
stupid, ugly, blond co-ed

When she told me about it
To your apartment I sped
After I saw you both come out
All I could see was red

Baby, you know with your vision
you can't see how a needle to thread
and besides that wasn't me
that was my roommate named Ted

To this accusation, again
not guilty I have pled
and all you talking about
is some old He Said, She Said

Well, my friend Lisa told me
that tomorrow you will wed
If it isn't true then why are
you hanging your sorry head

I knew you were immature
and your foolishness inbred
But for your sake I hope
my friend Lisa was misled

Girl, on this particular subject
lightly you better tread
I told you that you should have
quit while you were ahead

Yes, and its your friend Lisa
that tomorrow I will wed
'Cause I got so tired of you coming to me
with that old He Said, She Said!

Not My Style

When I first suspected
that on me
you were cheating
steadily

I would keep sleeping pills
close by so
that I could overdose
readily

For years now I
have overused
the defense mechanism
called denial

To face the truth
squarely, let me
tell you that was
not my style

I thought I was the angriest
with you when
I got so mad
I couldn't see

When some medicine fell out
of your pocket
and I could tell it was
for an STD

To put your business
on a billboard
I decided my reputation
it would defile

You better count
yourself lucky
Because that's just
not my style

When I realized you
couldn't be trusted
You know what
I thought at first

I was glad my uncle
had a funeral home
Because you were going
to need a big hearse

I confess I thought
of cutting up all
your clothes and putting
them in a pile

But again count
yourself lucky
Because you see that's
not my style

When you borrowed
that money from me
Saying "Everything
would be everything"

Didn't know when you
could pay me back,
then I found a receipt
for her wedding ring

34

I thought about
cooking you a meal
with that stuff for
cleaning bathroom tile

But you shouldn't
lose any sleep
Because you see that's
not my style

The thought that you
and I were engaged
must never have
entered your head

When you married
my very best friend
two days before we
were to be wed

Now I could have
taken steady aim
and shot you both
going down the aisle

Well you both
better be glad
That is just
not my style

I realize today, for
people like you
the universe
has a plan

And my best bet
was to step aside
and put everything
in God's hand

To hurt a loveless
lizard like you
would really not
be worth my while

You see I would have to
stoop as low as you
and that is definitely
not my style!

Don't Start None

I try to be
real pleasant
Always ready to
have some fun

Some people think
because I am nice
that over me,
they can run

Well, I must
issue a warning
and some of you
it may stun

I suggest that you
not mess with me
If you don't start none
won't be none

I try to be on
my best behavior
act like I have
a high income

I try my best
to get along
But I want you to
hear me everyone

Try to mess with
me, my man,
my daughter
or my son

Like I said in the
first off beginning
Don't start none
won't be none

Just 'cause I really
don't like to fight
Don't think that
I am a nun

Actually there was
a time in my past
that many a fight
I had won

So, if you try
to mess with me
everyone around
will come

It will be
a pitiful sight
so, don't start none
won't be none

Ya'll need to
hear me out
until you are sure
I am done

Excuse me but my
name is Big Bertha
So don't even try
to call me "hon"

I could just as
soon sit on you
some people say
I weigh a ton

So I'm telling you
one more 'gain
Don't start none
won't be none

You see, I try to
be like Dr. King
'Cause with nonviolence,
Peace can be spun

But there you go
trying to be smart
Now I gots to go
get my gun

Now when I put this
hurtin' on you
It can't be
easily undone

So, I'm telling you
your best bet is
Don't start none
won't be none

I'm trying my
best to convince
you of the
eventual outcome

If you mess with
any of my family
I mean, you better
know how to run

So when I'm trying
to be nice
Call me a
heroine unsung

Just don't
disrespect me
Don't start none
won't be none!

Parallel Lives

Two parallel lines never meet
unless one of them you bend

We live our lives in parallel
with no plans for this to end

Which one of us will bend?
Which one of us will bend?

Your work takes you in one direction
mine takes me in another

Instead of being like husband and wife
we act more like sister and brother

What you want for me would destroy
my soul, and leave me unfilled

In your wildest dreams you never thought
I'd be so strong-willed

What I want, but you cannot give,
is more than just respect

When I ask you to support my dream
you automatically object

Two parallel lines never meet
unless one of them you bend

We live our lives in parallel
with no plans for this to end

I don't care how much we pretend
I don't care how much we pretend

We entered this relationship
with all the wrong expectations

Before we realized it, we had
weathered many a tribulation

Something is very wrong, something
we don't know how to fix

But we never agreed on anything
not even when the kids were sick

Now we just go along, to get along
Being cordial and sometimes polite

We have no meaningful communication
So we don't know whose wrong or right

Two parallel lines never meet
Unless one of them you bend

We live our lives in parallel
with no plans for this to end

with no plans for this to end
with no plans for this to end

This Moment

We exploded into
each others lives
in this single moment

I knew I had found
the love of my life
in this precious moment

I held my breath
as you kissed me
in this special moment

I loved you more than I should
but not more than I could
in this exciting moment

You said whatever you had to say
to have me
at this stupid moment

I realized that everything you said
you meant only for
this brief moment

I realized that I was
your personal fool
for this ugly moment

I decided that love died
and I will never love again
from this very moment

What Do You Do?

What do you do
when you have wanted
All that you can want
and flaunted
All that you can flaunt
When you have pled
All that you can plead
and needed
All that you can need
and it isn't enough?

What do you do
when you have bent
All that you can bend
and lent
All that you can lend
When you have shown
All that you can show
and gone as far
as you can go
and it isn't enough?

What do you do
when you have dreamed
All that you can dream
and screamed
All that you can scream
When you have yelled
All that you can yell
and told
All that you can tell
and it isn't enough?

What do you do
when you have dealt
All that you can deal
and felt
all that you can feel
When you have feared
All that you can fear
and you have heard
All that you can hear
and it isn't enough?

What do you do
when you have thought
All that you can think
and drunk
All that you can drink
When you have bruised
All that you can bruise
and lost
All that you can lose
and it isn't enough?

What do you do
when you have forsaken
All that you can forsake
and taken
All that you can take
When you have tried
All that you can try
and cried
All that you can cry
and it isn't enough?

What do yo do
when you have said
all that you can say
and prayed
All that you can pray
When you have viewed
All that you can view
and done
All that you can do
and it isn't enough?

When you have hidden
all that you can hide
Ridden
All that you can ride

When you have phoned
all that you can phone
and moaned
All that you can moan

When you have lied
All that you can lie
and denied
All that you can deny

When you have believed
all that you can believe
and grieved
All that you can grieve

then
Leave
Just go on
and
Leave

Chapter Three

The Realization

In God's Time...

...You need to get your act together
before you go out of your mind

You need to

> Stop your meeting'
> Stop your cheatin'
> Stop your mistreatin'
> Stop your beatin'

'Cause everything happens
in God's Time

It happens

> in God's taste
> in God's reason
> in God's haste
> in God's season

Everything happens
in God's Time...

The Greatest Lie

You have lied to me
so often I thought
I would play this game
I would try to figure out
your greatest lie,
I could name

It might be the time
you called, said you'd be
over in a few
I saw you a few weeks
later and you asked
"What did you do?"

Or the time you bought
yourself a present you
really wanted to show me
But swore you didn't have
a dime of the thousands
you still owe me

Or maybe it was the time
we fought and you hit me
with the electric fan
You said it would be
the last time and then
you broke my hand

When I tried to convince
myself that you could
ever be anything else
I decided the greatest lie
ever told was the lie
I told myself!

You Change

Some how years can make you change
After a while you get tired
You begin to look again at your life
and the people you once admired

Somehow years can make you change
like when you first got fired
For just trying to do a good job
when others still on the job had retired

Somehow years can make you change
and one day you discover
that you are really not there
you are just someone's wife or mother

Somehow years can make you change
and you realized that you had to hover
over the children to get them raised
while trying not to smother

Somehow years can make you change
and you find yourself unfulfilled
and you cannot even remember
things about which you were thrilled

Somehow years can make you change
and your emotions one day spilled
Accepting the fact the power to change
is something you had been willed

Somehow years can make you change
You look in the mirror and see
If you don't claim the rest of your life
on your head only will it be

Somehow years can make you change
and you go on a shopping spree
When you first realize that
now you are actually free

Somehow years can make you change
when all of your children are grown
It's time for you to find "Happy"
That's somebody you've never known

Somehow years can make you change
and you find yourself on your own
You realize that the worse lonely
was when you were not alone

Somehow years can make you change
You see you have the worse health
You realize you've spent all of your life
Worrying about everyone else

Somehow years can make you change
all of your dreams are still on the shelf
You realize if you're going to be lonely
You might as well be lonely by yourself!

Somehow years can make you change

I Just Can't

One minute you want me
to feel sorry for you
The next you want to see
me hiding in fear
You used to keep me so upset
Now, I just can't
cry with that tear

Ain't no use of you shouting
and ranting about
What you are saying
to me is very clear
What you fail to realize is
I just can't
hear with that ear

Yeah, all the bad things
I used to see you do
once made me
just want to die
But go on and do what you wanna
'Cause, I just can't
see with that eye

You wanted me singing
in the kitchen
cutting up chicken
getting ready to fry
But you better get out of my face
'Cause I just can't
live with that lie

You vowed to have me
on the floor crawling
when you got
the kids custody
One thing you didn't quite count on
I just can't
bend with that knee

You thought you could get and
keep my self-esteem so low
that I would take
all this pain for free
But, my friends helped me to realize
I just can't
be in love with that me

I know you can't
quite comprehend
but some of this
I hope you can
You keep asking me for more and more
But, I just can't
give with that hand

Now, children, you know
that I am sorry
some day I hope
you will understand
I know how much you love your Daddy
But, I just can't
stay with that man!

Your Song

They say the very best writers
Only write about what they know
All we are putting on paper is what
the children of our families show

There are two sides to everything written
If our side puts you where you don't belong
It's because we cannot write your story
No, we cannot sing your song

We have borne some of your children
and raised them by ourself
Tried our best not to talk bad about you
and wouldn't let nobody else

So, if the picture we paint, you don't like
You feel it paints you like you're not that strong
Well, baby we cannot write your story
Brother man, we cannot sing your song

We have cooked some of you meals
Even darned and washed your clothes
Been with you through thick and thin
Listened to all of your cares and woes

With the load of our children we carry
Would you add to our list so long
No, we cannot write your story
No, we cannot sing your song

We have, on occasion, cleaned your house
Sometimes without having your name
We have loved you with all of our might
Even when we knew it was just a game

We loved you when we didn't love ourselves
Even after you were long gone
But we cannot write your story
No, we cannot sing your song

We have nursed you through crying spells
When you couldn't find a job
Getting caught with some white women
We helped to hide you from the mob

We are too busy validating our children
To play this emotional ping pong
You see, we cannot write your story
Forgive us, but, we cannot sing your song

You say you'll talk to us about it later
only your later never comes
We have gotten up to go to work everyday
while you have sat back on your thumbs

We are starring in this movie beside you
So to review it too, we can't go along
You see, we cannot write your story
Understand, we cannot sing your song

The Biggest Crumb

I am forever asking questions
and here's another one
As the larger parts are being eaten
Isn't the tiny piece left called the "crumb"

Well, if what you say is true
Then to me it seems kinda dumb
We let "the man" take off with the whole cake
while we fight over the "biggest crumb"

Now, I am sorry but the truth is
We have repeatedly succumb
to the devastating theory
known as the "biggest crumb"

Because of this strange mentality
just look at what we have become
a whole race of people killing each other
over the "biggest crumb"

No, on this particular subject
I will not stay mum
I can't stand the way we cuss
and fuss over the "biggest crumb"

Whenever I think about it
it makes me kinda numb
The way we sell our children and our
souls over the "biggest crumb"

Sometimes we get so desperate
at midnight here we come
Trying to steal from one another
the piece called the "biggest crumb"

It doesn't matter our station in life
or where we each came from
We let "them" take the lion's share
while we go to jail for the "biggest crumb"

Hey, you in that nice three-piece suit
Please don't look so glum
You know that what I'm saying is true
We've been worrying about the "biggest crumb"

I'm talking about Black people in business
who serve you chewing bubble gum
and stick you up with high prices
trying to get their piece of the "biggest crumb"

Why, we will even leave our families
and wind up being a bum
because we went off chasing
the illusion of the "biggest crumb"

Then we start nursing a bottle
of vodka, whiskey or rum
when we compare the real profits
to the size of the "biggest crumb"

Entire families, for generations
have sat back on their thumb
waiting on "the first" for the postman
to bring them their "biggest crumb"

We like to talk about people on welfare
while our grants we want "them" to fund
Hoping someone will approve
our proposal for the "biggest crumb"

Then there are artists, writers
and musicians with guitars they strum
While their agents, publicists, distributors
want ten per cent of their "biggest crumb"

The only thing that to me is worse
are the ministers who just sit and hum
through their little effort on Sunday, they want
a piece of someone else's "biggest crumb"

If we carefully do our addition
to me it seems in the final sum
I don't care how you slice it
"A CRUMB IS STILL A CRUMB"

If this slavery mentality goes unchallenged
the victory, "they have won"
The fat cats will keep getting fatter
while we fight over the "biggest crumb"

To get the message to Black people
we may need the African drum
Our time and talents are being exploited
while we are

settling,
stealing,
lying,

fighting,
killing,
dying,

over "THE BIGGEST CRUMB"

The Way It Is

To everyone along the feeding chain
artists are expected to make a contribution
If they do the most work, but receive the
least pay, isn't that prostitution?

Yes, challenging the way "The Man" has it
set up takes a little bravery
But, if someone hadn't been willing to make
a change, wouldn't we still have slavery?

All we hear is "that's the way it is"
when we challenge the status quo
But if somebody hadn't challenged the system
wouldn't we still have Jim Crow?

In order to right a terrible wrong
someone must be willing to move mountains
If someone hadn't had that type of courage,
wouldn't we have separate drinking fountains?

To change the way things are structured
someone has to stand up and take note
Look at those willing to die for their beliefs
so that we could have the right to vote

When something is very wrong, you've got to
make changing it your "biz"
and promise yourself you will never accept
the answer, "That's just the way it is"

Chapter Four

The Celebration

In God's Time...

...You still wretching and agonizing
Seems like you, I need to remind

So you can

>   Stop your sighin'
>   Stop your denying
>   Stop your lyin'
>   Stop you cryin'

'Cause everything happens
in God's time

It happens

>   in God's race
>   in God's power
>   in God's grace
>   in God's hour

Everything happens
in God's Time...

Black Beauty

Black Beauty

Why are you sitting
there all alone?

Don't you know you should be
sitting on a throne

Black Beauty

Why do you want to
run and hide?

Don't you know you should
walk with a queenly pride

Black Beauty

Why don't you
know your worth?

Don't you know you are
the mother of this earth

Black Beauty

Why don't you
let anyone in?

Don't you know you should be
proud of the color of your skin

Black Beauty

Why are you afraid
to speak out loud?

Don't you know you have a history
of which you can be proud

Black Beauty

Don't you know that you should
love yourself?

Even though your history
isn't in the books on the shelf

Black Beauty

Why aren't you
going to school?

That teacher had no business
calling you a fool

Black Beauty

Why are you
about to cry?

Don't you know your self-esteem does
not have to die

Black Beauty

Why do you still have
a sad frown?

I know our generation
has let you down

Black Beauty

Why are you still out
there in the cold?

Don't you know you
have a hand to hold

Black Beauty

Why the sad look
on your face?

Don't you know you're entitled
to all of God's grace

Black Beauty

Why don't you feel
any better?

Don't you know we adults
will get our act together

Out Of My Life

People say I need to leave this man
He's really bringing me down
But every time I think about leaving
or staying my head begins to pound

I told him good-bye as I packed my bags
and was heading out of the door
He laughed and said I would be back
'Cause I didn't know how to live "pore"

I can't believe I didn't let myself call
and it has been an entire day
but I wonder how late tonight at work
he will have to stay

I am so proud of me, I have not tried
to reach him, and it's been a week
I wonder when I run into him now
will he try to speak

Okay, it's been a month now
and I am starting to believe
that I can live without him
but I wonder how long will I grieve

It has been a whole year now
and I am so pleased with me
I'll admit I almost called him once
No one told me how lonely free could be

I'll admit that I still think of him
But he was all wrong for me
He would always call me out of my name
then I'd let him walk on my dignity

I am doing everything I can to keep
my self esteem from going too low
I've made it! I got him OUT OF MY LIFE
and back I will never go!

He's gone for good, I'm no longer afraid
I've stopped sleeping with my knife
Without him always putting me down
Now I can make something OUT OF MY LIFE!

'Bout to Get

You thought that
you had stopped me
But all you did
was slow me down

I needed the extra
time to decide how
you, I could
go around

You thought that
all my joy away
from
me you
had taken

But I am pleased
to inform you
that you are sadly
mistaken

Now that I am
living my life
the way God
recommends

You see I'm
"'bout to get"
all the blessings
my God intends

You thought that
you had hurt me
beyond all
repair

But the hurt you
inflicted reminded me,
how much Joy
should be there

You thought you had
wounded me enough
to cause me
never to feel

But I needed to feel that pain
to distinguish between
what is false
and what is real

Now that I am
living my life
the way my God
can be proud

You see, I'm
"'bout to get"
All the happiness
that is allowed

You thought that
you had ruined
all my chances
for success

But I learned
that dealing
with you was
just another test

You thought that
you had stifled
all my
creativity

But you have just
multiplied it ten times
over through all
this adversity

Now that I'm
living my life
strictly by
God's book

You see I'm
"'bout to get"
so much goodness
I can't look!

You 'bout to get
10 to 20 for the
years of beating
on me, your wife

But I can't worry
about that 'cause
I'm, "'bout to get"
back my life

You are
"'bout to get"
exactly what
you deserved

I hear they got
a room down there,
that's hot and
for you it's reserved

But now that I'm
living my life
the way my God
has shown

You see that I'm
"'bout to get"
more love than
I have ever known

You Don't Live Here

I wish I could get back
all the nights I lived in fear
and the money I spent on
surgery for my middle ear

I wish I had my memory back
from the time death was so near
and all those days in intensive care
hooked up to that life support gear

I wish I could get back
the water from each and every tear
and all those days of unhappiness
I mean, each and every year

I wish I had all the items you used to throw
like all those bottles of beer
and I wish I had money for all the looks
you gave me that were queer

I wish I could recapture the
days of living behind that veneer
and I wish I could wave a wand and
make all this guilt disappear

But it feels good to know that
my life you no longer steer
and to think that you were someone
I once used to revere

Well, you can stop giving me that look
how well I know that leer
That's right don't look back
I mean don't even peer

Because we are about to have a party
a celebration, my dear
We are celebrating the one thing
that could make my family cheer

For the occasion I bought me a present,
a sweater of pure cashmere
when I finally realized that I can
get on with my career

What you pay in child support
truly a pittance mere
Is not being used for this party
nor my cake with an extra tier

I have changed all the locks
even to the gate in the rear
Because we are celebrating the fact
that from now on YOU DON'T LIVE HERE!

The Gingerbread Woman

You have attempted
very courageously

to define my existence
permanently

You have signed and sealed
my fate anonymously

and expect me to accept
it graciously

You have decided there
are places that I shouldn't be

Your halls, hallowed by
white supremacy

I'm the Gingerbread Woman
and with all your trickery

You caught my brother
but you can't catch me

If you had taken time
to learn my history

I don't think that
surprised you would be

You see I am from
a long rich dynasty

Of African kings and queens
of true royalty

In Africa and America
I have joint tenancy

but how I succeed to you
is still a mystery

I'm the Gingerbread Woman
and with all your trickery

You caught my brother
but you can't catch me

I have nursed the children
of the world at my knee

From my womb sowed the seeds
of peace and harmony

I have fed the poor and
hungry unselfishly

While raising my own
strong Black family

I have talents that
you will never see

To my hopes and dreams
you do not hold the key

Because I'm the Gingerbread Woman
and with all my trickery

You caught my brother
but you can't catch me

I have been jailed
without bars for you to see

Without a trial or the
offer of clemency

I know how confinement feels
when it's solitary

When no one understands or
cares actually

I grow weary of having to prove
myself and I mean daily

When the same is not demanded of people
less qualified than me

But I'm the Gingerbread Woman
and with all your trickery

You caught my brother
but you can't catch me

For years you have abused
and taken from me

Everything you could extract,
all my creativity

I am telling you this
at my first opportunity

To get my talents now
there will be a fee

I have found enormous strength
and an inner beauty

With a finely honed instinct
to protect my sanity

But I'm the Gingerbread Woman
and with all your trickery

You caught my brother
but you can't catch me

If I am stopped in one career
I will change spontaneously

I will wait tables, scrub floors
or dig ditches shamelessly

I will paint a picture, hook a rug
or write books of poetry

Before I give credence to your
thoughts about me

I guess you are wondering by now
how I keep my positivity

It is my faith in God
and my sense of victory

And I'm the Gingerbread Woman
and with all your trickery

You caught my brother
but you can't catch me!

I Can Give

I woke up this morning
with an ache in my heart
I found that I had only
existed in part

I could not give
I could only receive
Such a lesson to learn
I could not believe

I met a child walking
down the street
I gave him a dollar to
get something to eat

I did not feel a thing
from this generous act
I vowed to try once again
with myself I made a pact

I put an extra ten dollars
in the church plate
'Cause the preacher said he'd
make sure that the homeless ate

I felt better for a moment
and then I sat and thought
It wouldn't be very much
that my ten dollars bought

I still felt maybe I
was only half alive
that I was just holding on
Just trying to survive

I went to my closet
and took out my old clothes
and gave them to a shelter
who would get them heaven knows

I thought maybe taking time
to give those old things to someone
But it didn't make me feel better
when this deed was done

Then I saw a young boy crying
because he couldn't read
and I worked with him everyday
until me, he did not need

The lesson I have learned
on this very day, you know
Is a lesson I should have
learned a long time ago

The feeling I got that day
I can't explain to anybody else
That day I learned "To Give"
is to give of oneself

My heart is finally whole
I no longer feel like a sieve
I am so grateful because
Now I can give, Now I can live

Chapter Five

The Spiritualization

In God's Time...

...In order for you to be convinced
He will always give you a sign

So you can

  Stop your poutin'
  Stop your toutin'
  Stop your shoutin'
  Stop your doubtin'

'Cause everything happens
in God's Time

It happens

  in God's pace
  in God's might
  in God's embrace
  in God's sight

Everything happens
In God's Time

There Is A Gift

Every child can't be first or second
Even third, fourth or fifth
But in each and every child
There is a gift

Every child cannot be strong
Each child cannot be swift
But know that inside each child
There is a gift

Every child cannot be "perfect"
Even the one who seems adrift
But even in that angry child
There is a gift

At first, we may not see it
Layers of pain we may have to lift
But underneath we will always find
There is a gift

We must loosen up our minds
and not always be so stiff
Raise our expectations
or we may miss "their gift"

We can improve our world
whole races we can uplift
If we remember, that in every child
There is a gift!

A Garden Out Back

I'm 82 and pretty healthy
and very proud of that fact
How did I manage to live so long
and keep myself intact?

Well, it really ain't no secret
I can tell you the reason exact
Wherever Life's winds blew me
I just put me a little garden out back

Before I could plant me some tomatoes
they would bring me dirt in a sack
Then I'd plant me some peppers and squash
and some cucumbers in a straight tract

I takes my vitamins, drinks my water
and juices from my vegetables I extract
and I gets all the exercise I need
tending to my little garden out back

I tries to get enough rest
I don't eat nothing that has no fat
I turns off that old TV
and piles my newspapers in a stack

But some questions have occurred to me
at night while laying flat
How many of our problems could be solved
If we just put a little garden out back

Like how many people could stop pretending
that they are not really Black
and how many true friends could they
really then start to attract

How many people could stop taking
that Valium and all that Prozac
If they just took the time to plant
them a little garden out back

I wonder how many young people
wouldn't be strung out on all that crack
How many teens wouldn't need to be in gangs
and old people, like me, they attack

How many families could we strengthen
and then keep them intact
If everyone just had them
a little garden out back

How many people wouldn't need to buy
their clothes from the next larger rack
and how much food for the homeless
would we really lack

How many fewer laws would
we actually need to enact
If it was a law that people must
have a little garden out back

No Color

I have noticed one thing
in my travels
as I go from town to town

Pain can be packaged
in beautiful shades
of yellow, white and brown

Once that package is
opened, one thing
I have always found

PAIN HAS NO COLOR

when someone is
lying there
on the ground

I have thought about
this often, as I move
from state to state

There are few things
that separate us
and those we agitate

If we could stop for
just one minute
and really contemplate

PAIN HAS NO COLOR

When we see the
victim has just
been raped

I see this phenomenon
all the time as I travel
from one city to another

We worry about the wrong things
that's why we can't get along
with each other

If we could just spend
more time listening instead
of always talking under cover

PAIN HAS NO COLOR

When it's a baby
someone has
tried to smother

I continue to wonder
everyday as I fly
across this nation

What we need to do to get
more people to understand
this situation

It would seem we would
focus on what unites us
instead of more separation

PAIN HAS NO COLOR

When the child is
a victim of
sexual molestation

PAIN HAS NO COLOR

I Didn't Get

I didn't get to tell you
how much you mean to me
and how sorry I am that your
life had to have such misery

I know that you are gone now
I understand it was God's choice
but what I wouldn't give
just to hear your voice

The days crawl by so slowly
I can barely eat or sleep
I'm doing the least I can to get by
because I am hurting so deep

I know that you are gone now
I understand it is God's grace
but what I wouldn't give
just to see your face

Nights almost seem to stand still
As thoughts of you flood my room
I know you wouldn't want me to be sad
but my heart cannot shake this gloom

I know that you are gone now
I understand it is God's plan
But what I wouldn't give
just to hold your hand

I didn't get to tell you
of all my hopes and dreams
To understand your philosophy
and to see what to you life means

I know that you are gone now
I understand it is God's gain
But what I wouldn't give
not to feel this pain

I didn't get to tell you
how much I want to be like you
To have your integrity, gentle ways
and some of your wisdom, too

I know that you are gone now
I understand it is God's time
But I can't understand why He took
your life instead of mine

I didn't get to tell you
how much I love you so
I think of the things we didn't
get to do, because you had to go

I know that you are gone now
I understand this is God's test
But what I wouldn't give
to know your soul's at rest

Just A Dream

Each time that I lay
down to sleep
there's this recurrent theme

Which visits me
each and every night
As I begin to dream

It is to have a world
Where things are
really as they seem

And everyone works
together like they
are on a "special team"

To make a world that's
safe for children
to play along the stream

And not to have to worry
some relative or stranger
will make them scream

And to have homes for
everybody with floors
so shiny they gleam

With enough food on
the table, bowls filled
with peaches and cream

There would be a blanket
of caring woven
without a single seam

And adults with faces
all aglow because they
would have good self esteem

Each time that I awake
I try to
remember this scene

Because in the real
world outside my door
is another dope fiend

I can't begin to tell you
some of the
stuff I have seen

Daddies and boyfriends
both treating
their women so mean

Babies on my block being born
to mothers still
in their teens

And newborns off alcohol
and drugs like cocaine
they have to be weaned

At times I am very glad
that my imagination
is so keen

Because sometimes
I just like to pretend
that I am really a queen

And not to worry if I
am never full
It is popular to be lean

I can just
summon "Jack"
with this cold pinto bean

Well, It's night
again now
Back to my idea supreme

That love and
kindness were found
in everybody's gene

I must now unzip
the night and crawl
back into my world pristine

It's too bad
it's really only
just a dream

A Million Black Men

On a beautiful sunnny day
in early fall

There was a sight for sore eyes
both large and small

For as far as the eye could see
Black men did sprawl

From the Capital steps to
the Lincoln Memorial so tall

A history making event
and well organized overall

There were over A MILLION BLACK MEN
on that Washington Mall

They came by buses, planes
and cars that did stall

To get there some marched
and some would have even crawled

They came from across this country
some even had a southern drawl

From Los Angeles to England
from the Carribean to St Paul

To recommit to family
Rid their world of drugs and alcohol

Over a MILLION BLACK MEN
answered Farrakhan's call

There was singing and dancing,
speeches that did enthrall

The men stood there all day
except those leaning against the wall

They were not demanding Justice
or watching a game of football

But were praying for ATONEMENT
for one and for all

A more solid display of UNITY
no one could recall

Over A MILLION BLACK MEN
on that Washington Mall

A million single dollars waving
made some doubters squall

Some still want to pretend no good
can come of this at all

A new group of Black leaders
were duly installed

All singing and preaching
had died down by night fall

The men hugged and dispersed
no fighting, not one brawl

with over A MILLION BLACK MEN
on that Washington Mall

To discredit this event some Blacks
tried to have the gall

That anyone could find fault
had to appall

From the Park Service count
that was ridiculously small

To the not so surprising
media coverage stall

These men could not be stopped
As they entered God's hall

Over A MILLION BLACK MEN
on that Washington Mall!

On The Other Side

On the other side of Gloom
Joy has a room
On the other side of Wrong
Right has a song

On the other side of Alone
Happiness has a home
On the other side of night
There's a beautiful day light

Just on the other side

On the other side of Survive
is the joy of being Alive
On the other side of Rain
is a Rainbow so plain

On the other side of Denied
is a strength you cannot hide
On the other side of Confused
is Truth waiting to be used

Just on the other side

On the other side of Deceive
There is someone you can believe
On the other side of Sadness
Make way for some Gladness

On the other side of "Can't Cope"
There is always Hope
On the other side of Sorrow
There is always Tomorrow

Just on the other side